Polder

CHRIS MCCULLY was born in Bradford and now lives and works in the Netherlands, where he writes poems, textbooks and works on fly-fishing and gives freelance courses on aspects of using the English language. For many years he was a full-time academic in the UK, and he remains chairman and co-director of the Modern Literary Archives programme at the John Rylands University Library in Manchester. Chris McCully travels widely, making up to a dozen overseas trips a year in order to write features for the fly-fishing press in the UK and Netherlands.

CHRIS McCULLY

Polder

CARCANET

Acknowledgements

'An Auction for Amsterdam' was among the runners-up in the 2004 Cardiff International Poetry Competition, and appeared in *New Welsh Review*. Other poems here appeared in *Critical Quarterly*, *PN Review*, *Poetry Wales*, *New Welsh Review* and *Staple*. I am grateful to the editors of these publications for permission to reprint the poems in this collection. A further acknowledgement is due to Em. Querido's Uitgeverij B.V., Amsterdam, for kind permission to include an adaptation of Hendrik Marsman's poem 'Herinnering aan Holland' (here given the title 'Mindful of Holland'). Professor Bernard Comrie, of the Max Planck Institute for Evolutionary Anthropology in Leipzig, kindly allowed me to make use of some of his linguistic examples in 'Remembering Indo-European'. 'Ithaka', first published in *Poetry Wales*, has been set for contralto and piano by the composer Karl Magnuson. I am also most grateful to Grevel Lindop, Rob Rollison, Fergus Wilde and Agada Ammeraal for the criticism and advice given to me during the drafting of some of the pieces.

First published in Great Britain in 2009 by
Carcanet Press Limited
Alliance House
Cross Street
Manchester M2 7AQ

A CIP catalogue record for this book is available from the British Library
ISBN 978 1 84777 017 2

The publisher acknowledges financial assistance from Arts Council England

Typeset by XL Publishing Services, Tiverton
Printed and bound in England by SRP Ltd, Exeter

Contents

I

Dust

Dust

I have looked into dust.

Dust is in the Bechstein, the dahlias are dust, the stray horse under its clouded moon is dust. All the somewheres where everyone once was combed the future for someone in particular and found nothing but dust. The elderly schoolmasters and piano-teachers are dust, and the leaves of the piano primer were eaten, note by note, by dust. Dust is in the Venice piazzas, and the bed full of sunlight is dying of drifted skin that has already become dust. There was dust in the air under the airplane wing, dust under the thumbtack, dust in the fingernail. The exercise books and student notes aim towards dust until they burst in a cloud of smoke, a censer and a thwarted hosanna, where dust covers the choir-stall, and the cope of farewell.

Age shall not wither her, nor shall it weary them, whoever she was and whoever they are, but age was already in the first thought of weariness, because there was dust – dust in the billet, dust at the cenotaph, dust in the greenroom, dust in the hymn book, dust in the piano-stool and the abandoned ashtray.

As I say, I have looked into dust.

★ ★ ★ ★

There are others who will speak to you about the sea, the sea. Not I. Others will write to you about the loss that everyone was and the griefs that are in every change of key. Not me. There are even the distinguished voices of the agonised that will show you fear in a handful of dust, but that isn't the dust I mean, beloved. And there are those from the future who will, with a calm sneer, inform you tomorrow that everything becomes the night. But that's not right.

I'll tell you about dust.

You have the memories. You have the Insta-Snaps in bundles, the framed photographs of weddings propped on the television. You have the television. You have the presents of the lost faces, the travelling rug from Istanbul, the blue Greek carpet in the bathroom, the unframed icon made by an Albanian itinerant, the occasional table gifted to you by a one-legged carpenter whose life was already over. You have the radio that someone bought you six birthdays ago. Yes, you think you have memories – the indiscreet peelings of underwear, the mouth whose tongue erected you from the lees of the Burgundy; you have the letters of the mouth bundled in a whisky crate at the back of the closet. And you can't bear to open the whisky, the letters, the memories. This is because you haven't inherited memories. You have inherited... Dust? No. It isn't yet quite dust. You have inherited childhoods, all of them yours.

★ ★ ★ ★

'Childhood?' you'll say, not appearing to welcome this tacit invitation to think about yourself. 'But I'm not my childhood. Well, I'm not... I'm hardly... a child. I may retain parts of the child I was once but...'

You're thinking about this the wrong way.

Childhood is not the endless recitation of the past, where the past repeats itself by rote and rhythm like a Latin declension until eventually the voice falters at exactly the place where the fist was raised, and insistent fingers shook tomorrow by its throat. *Amo, amas, amat; mensa, mensa, mensam; dominus, domine, dominum.* Doh-re-mi. The first true note just happens to be *amo.*

But as you point out, you have changed. The language isn't the same, the declensions has lost their inflections and the rhythm has run into the hiatus of its own failures.

Elsewhere, someone is practising scales.

I don't want to invoke the shibboleths of the analyst's couch − can't you see the dust falling through the sunlight as the sunlight opens like mother in the eyes of the heavy brocade curtains? I'm not summoning the demons of betrayal, the poisons of untruth and distance, the reasons for an altered life.

You have changed. You've shed many skins. Your previous imago is an endless set of shucks. I wonder if you've ever wondered where the skins go? No? Not onto the fencepost like the leavings of a giant insect that has outgrown the nutrients of its incipient life? Not into the nugatory shards in the wasteland? No? No fragments, not even a nail-paring, to shore against your ruin? No?

No − the tacit No that began when childhoods became dust. It became the reason why you find it difficult to remember the face of the name where all the accusations had to begin. Dust glazed the photograph. The inner raptus of memory began to peel away in sunburn. Face it: the leavings were all over the house. Where did all the dust come from – the dust under the piano, the smear on the skirting-board, the grey glaze under the bathroom mirror, the tufts of drift under the bed?

It's skin.

It is technically only skin, the set of all the days of skin you have outgrown and will keep outgrowing beyond, beloved, the day you are no longer conscious of skin. Where did you think the nail-parings went? Where the hard skin and the verruca, the treated wart? Where the snuff-dry hay in the stable and the blasted rose? Where the scurf in the curry-comb? And the withered dahlias? And the black spray of so many questions?

D'you love me	*Dust*
Do you still love me	*Dust*
Is it all right	*Dust*
Who was she	*Dust*
Will it ever be	*Dust*
Is there a future	*Dust*
Will you ever	
Do you remember	*Dust*
Your lover	*Dust*
Do you still love me	

It will always be dust.

★ ★ ★ ★

Where do the days begin? The unreal slaver of the poet's sea? What does a look at the moon encounter? Where does the dandruff come from? The ash in the wind? Where does the bonfire go?

Where do you think the dust in the house called Sorry came from? A casual exhaust fume? The passing remnants of clouds speeding summer as it passed? The scab in the armpit of a gondolier? It came from you, and the cycle of shedding solitudes.

You became without your solitude, and left dust.

★ ★ ★ ★

We're thick with it, under the airplane wing, under the penumbra of Los Angeles smog, on the lamps in the brothels of Piraeus and Delhi. Dust in the streetlamps; dust in the snow. Whirled with violence round about the pendant world, like a muff of gravity. Where does it all come from? Where everyone must go.

But who knows where dust began, and where the epic of drift will end? What first mote was in whose first eye, where was somewhere, and when was somewhere anywhere?

★ ★ ★ ★

I have looked into dust.

The first mote was beyond space or time. It was a word but it was beyond a word. It was an infinite point of density in No-time, in the beginning before the beginning was. It wasn't even yet a thought.

And there in the first mote was the first dust of all the worlds that had been before No-time – dust of castles, of extinct elephants, of the remaining snuff of eminent literary editors, of the nuclear fume from distant suns, of pumice stones and ejected pomegranate seeds, of popes, pan-scrubs, bank-managers, billets, the dispersed lava of a million volcanoes, of the dried tears of maimed marriages, relics of another explosion. It was the billionth shard, the ten trillionth husk. It was the catch in the throat that comes just before the childhood of the lover's heartbreaking, perennial cry: Be what I want, not what you need.

Be what I want, not what you need.

It's the cry in the faces of the wedding photographs that stare back at you from their unanointed places on top of the television. Dust blinds the stares.

But the cry doesn't know itself as a cry. Perhaps it never did, and had merely gathered into an infinitely dense, infinitely heavy point composed of all the cries of all the lovers of the worlds. It had collapsed into dust, and endlessly collapsing, became a mote.

Gravity, beloved. It was all collapsing, like the weight in the air of a lung. Something was breathing. Dust was the breath of the gods.

And in the breath, a mote. In the beginning, before the beginning was, since there could be no beginning since whatever was breathing couldn't be conscious of a beginning. Where does a breath begin and end? With the remnant of the last pulmonary stroke? Or the beginning of the next?

And there was the mote of the worlds.

★ ★ ★ ★

Out it all came, accelerating into solitudes and disconsolation, and all the somewheres that were still to be. Out came the rivers, the birds' nests, the stories; out came the cutlery and the manicure sets; out came the tired children and the exhausted lovers, not knowing whose was which. Out came the elephants and iguanas; out came the alcoholics and the bishops; out came the doers of good works and those who simply wanted a cigarette; out came the arks and the doctors; out came Venice; out came Michelangelo and Milton, each looking surprised. Out came Beethoven, seeming furious. Out came the mothers and the analysts, the accusations and the prophets; out came the suicides and the wedding photographs; the in-trays and the dead letter drops; out came people called Cheryl and Steve, Emma and Anthony, Wolfgang and Anastasia, and two sisters looking for a wild horse. Out came the grey smear of dawn over city skylines, and a nest of spiders. Out came the blood of a summer afternoon. Out came the Latin declensions. Out dropped a clouded moon; out came the Goldberg Variations and the airline attendants; out came a Bechstein; out came a piano stool and a pair of arthritic hands. Out came a boy; out came a bed with bloodstained sheets, and lovers' letters. Out came the goodbyes and all the voices of all the children that would be dust in the house called Sorry.

A later age than this will inspect the disaster through telescopes and infra-red imaging, and call it a brief history of time.

★ ★ ★ ★

And out came the voice that is this, now, from the universal explosion, whose background radiation you can still hear in the dial of the radio and still see in the afterglow of the switched-off television. And that voice too will be dust, and dust again the voices of the pages and the voices of the lovers.

For a while it will hold together. Gravity, beloved. History is heavy with dust. But something is breathing, always beyond consciousness or witness, and in time, through times beyond witness, the dust will begin to gather, and lie again in the dahlias and the cricket pavilions, and settle in the air of sunlit afternoons in Berlin; and the Venetian piazzas will slowly sink under its weight, century after century, where not even this voice – which is yours, beloved – will be waiting, since the waiting will have become the movement of dust; and the voices and the radios, the air-conditioners, the aspirations, the minor odysseys of the broken heart will become for an instant, and then will have been, and will all have been dust.

II

Polder

Over and Out

You will not write poems
any more. This
is a poem
that says
so

Polder

It was born from waving, from sand islands
disappearing into mist, from the goodbyes
to the ships with their freight of expensive religion
vanishing towards the Baltic, a fret of masts
like rigged needles disappearing into the sea.

How, then, to maintain, how sustain
watertight Holland, guilty but ingenious,
against the nails of the north wind
and the narrows of the night-watch
or inundations of the day?

This is the answer beyond farewell, Godspeed –
more about puddings than metaphysics:
Protestant pumping-stations, the low machinery
turning fathom to mulch, mulch to pasture...
Not scenery, but reclamation.

And yet it dreams of waves.
A ship was its ambition.

Mindful of Holland

Hendrik Marsman's famous poem 'Herinnering aan Holland' is still learned by heart by every Dutch schoolchild.

Thinking on Holland
I see wide rivers
flowing slowly
through an endless map;
high rows of surprising
poplars plying –
feathers at the edge
of the horizon's nap.
And in the pouring
space, deep-lying
farmsteads drift
through distances
of copse and village,
nubs of towers,
churches, elm-trees –
ancient intricacies.
Here's low-hanging light,
but the sun gradually
in mist's grey difference
being smothered, obscured;
and in all the counties
the voice of the water
repeating disaster
being feared, overheard.

Islands

If you wanted to build an island
would you plant a tree, and wait
from its tap-root to its heavy lace
of lungs and leaves a century?

The wind couldn't purchase the soil
that was grown from sand, and there
from buoyant air and the indignant gulls'
squall of uncertainty there would be land.

To fasten the fen you would hew
for rainwater back, and cut
from salt-stricken loam three fields to plough
while the wounds on your hands turned black.

The shoe of night and the spade
to bury the dead; the prayer
for construction to end and for peace
to release the vice in your head:

they built what you wanted, an island,
from the one tree's root, and now
you hold in your injured hands the scales,
the sail-cloth and the bitter fruit.

It's for others you reclaimed an island.
You watch it float past, unmoored
from your making, into the dark
that no longer means you. Nor will it last.

Remembering Indo-European

The man cried.
The man died.
The man killed the woman.
I am ashamed of my brother.
The wolf is bad.

The man whose son is working,
the woman with whom I had lunch...
You lied knowingly.

The men went.

He is a farmer.
I got up early and went for a walk.
The wolf is bad.
He is singing.

...to whom you forgive...
...he took me...
...drunkard...
...father, my father...

He went into the house where my brother lives.
The men stood by the hut from which the woman had come.
Soon in front of us appeared a village which we did not know.

The Thorn Carol

I tried to get home, but couldn't find the place:
Fell-side, caul water; trees filled with grace;
A string of cold blossom; ironwork below
The green-stained barb of the hawthorn-O.

I searched along footsteps from years before.
They led to someone else's door.
I asked for directions. There was nowhere to go
But the green-stained barb of the hawthorn-O.

I tracked down the map of myself for a key
To the lock that was missing. What was missing was me.
I yelled for remission, in the air and snow.
The reply was the barb of the hawthorn-O.

I went through nine cities, through the knocking shops,
To the end of the bottle when the music stops,
Looked in the letters and the rain's brilliant bow
For the green-stained barb of the hawthorn-O.

Lately a scholar, whose cavil was called hearse,
Lately a book in its powers… They curse
The distance of lamplight whose edges grow
The green-stained barb of the hawthorn-O.

I want to get home but I don't know where.
The taxi-driver set fire to my hair.
The trains ran down darkness, the rivers didn't flow
Past the green-stained barb of the hawthorn-O.

I hungered the winter, had winter's voice.
I shouldn't have come back here but I had no choice:
The starving rain-drop; the bricks fed with snow;
And the green-stained barb of the hawthorn-O.

A Curtal at Old Year's Eve

Early or overnight earth's turned to snow.
The heron eyes a garden pond,
untidy hackles wasting its neck.
The bamboo rides inside the wind.

Fret, fret, fret in the full grey sky.
You'll do more digging come the spring.
There is no winter left to wreck.

Murdering the Sea

to a child

Why there are windmills is because
they fought the sea, the *rijk*
of herring-gull, the whale's-way,
the slow struggle of the anemone –

lifted it in sailcloth arms
throttled for sky, and ate the wave
till here where you are could burn,
and the ploughshare come dry.

As far as you look is artifice
or put to work: the air
fills oyster shells with snow; you're borne
by weeks of earth and ice; and deep
under the Amsteldijk carp sleep.

A Walk to Kleine Loopveld

Feathers are frozen to the ice,
a fret of shavings yesterday,
and today, January motionless –
even the skater's blade; even your breath.
A fox has been at work here.

You come to trust what hurt
the winterkill of Holland, and its weight
will bear skaters and the coot's ripped throat
as far as thaw, where upside-down
alike the ice and carcase float.

Camellia

There's always ice to come, and always ice
contains the intricate

Camellia: such crimson engineering,
filaments that fuse into a globe, an eye
of coral ruched into the frost.
It stares you back through valves of silk,
has opened, opened, will be opening –
aspected, simultaneous.
And yet there's always ice.

When for Anyone

When your bones are chalk and everyone's gone
and it's too cold to go out, too dangerous
in all the traffic and the grift of ice;
when you don't understand what's in the can
and why there's so much more to think about
if only the insurance covered it;
when there are strangers with professional eyes
and you have no idea of quantities
and cooking such a chore, you're always one;
when darkness...
          ...But you leave the radio on
for company and what about your will
and the bed-linen hurts and your piss is a rope
drawing a needle for night, until
for anyone you're only an album, or
inches for footsteps, fearing the slope

On Greenfield Station

The signal's down and the weekend rains.
The blossom's flattened: translucent stains.
Nowhere to go. Nothing to do.
And has the express come through?

You paid for the glebe, and for temperance.
The day went on dancing, but you didn't dance.
You missed the timing, the steps weren't true.
And has the express come through?

You shelled for marriages, and for the wakes.
The hurling sky broke into headaches
while you broke into distance; but the journeys weren't due.
And has the express come through?

You bought the irony, wore the jokes
like a shiny suit. It impressed the folks –
but whose were the words you said you knew?
And has the express come through?

You don't understand the sky at night.
The trees have no names, the birds sing from spite.
Still, these miracles don't believe in you.
And has the express come through?

You thought this was home. It was just a place
you never quite stopped for, the dismantled face
of a left-over question with nothing to do.
And has the express come through?

An Auction for Amsterdam

That man, who recently acquired –
        for an astronomical price –
        the old Dutch master,
I wish him well, I wish him well.
It turns out that this hitherto-neglected, until-now-
        unattributed piece of transcendent
        Biblical hokum
wasn't anyone's to sell.

Imagine avarice, locked in
        its 22nd-floor office with its Dic-
        taphone and its cruel secretary,
its bank of screens, its plasm of phones.
Hands crook round the Eagle atop the walking-frame,
        but nothing moves except the brightening eyes
        that get their promises to keen
among a nest of deals and bones.

And what's he bought, that man? A prophet
        in a 17th-century, Thank-God-I've-made-it pose:
        I travelled, then studied Greek; then put that by for guilders.
        Now here I am. Now here I am.
Nonesuch, I sit and watch them every day. They move in
        rimless glasses, architects of coffee, raincoats, air,
        on any street that crawls the smell of drains
in Amsterdam, in Amsterdam.

To the last most intricate detail, they too
        have wives wear sharpened scissors, dirty toenails;
        down to the valves and palp, breasts and bush consumed:
mute need; burnt night. And then the night
whose ochre grumbles as it pays, or scratches
        stub-ends of its brush. The technicalities of skin admire,
        geometry of moon betray –
and bleed them white, and bleed them white.

And what the eyes just paid for is this
     culture that means everywhere, yet is no one's –
     a finicking insistence on the peripheral, pathetic, over-obvious
                                        bowl
of withered flowers; the starveling dog.
These things are home, they nag between the tapestries,
     dust falls and lies, whatever light. While outside… Outside…
     Perhaps he knows, the man who rooked the master. If so,
he bought the fog. He bought the fog.

Minoan

You imagine them speaking
In a broken row of exclamation marks
Whose purpose was a temple;

Striking at the heat; brazing the clay;
Moving each autumn to apprehend a god
Whose justice was a pasture,

Whose cattle grazed
The celestial hieroglyphs;
Whose jealousies were stars.

Plug in the lights, the electricity!
Night is, and the Hunter,
And the sea rising.

Pronouns

Is it just me?
The problem of the pronoun *We*
Won't go away.
You try to circumvent it by
An artful *I*,
And yet
I bet
For all your using *I*'s
You generalise
Your plural self to the extent
That it were *We*
Your *I* had meant.
Therefore despite the *I*'s you use
It's *We* you choose,
Or possibly
It's *We* you can't choose to ignore.
Is that what *I*'s a pronoun for?
Or is it me?

Caribbean Shorts

Spanish cigarettes;
wet heat; perpetual transits
heading for New York.

★

Tropic green on fire,
gri–gri falls in bills of flame:
dollars burn witchcraft.

★

Lime–twists, sugar–salt –
slaked thirst, shanty; hurricane…
The petrol's breathing.

The Bough

A tree's not utterly
a tree until you see
through how you see the tree:

the acorns, corbels, and
the loam of leaves amend
themselves meanwhile. Intend

an oak, and it is all
the oaks, whose radical
endowment is the fall

that also made the snow
forming the radial bough
to be the eye you grow:

and how anew
there is no Now.

Eating the Spring

It's bloody spring, the urgency
of green and left undone.
Cleavages disconcertingly
shake nipples at the sun

Meanwhile, meanwhile... The stricken spars
of crocus fret the day
and ash-buds burn like Marmite jars
among the boughs of may

Looking at Orion

Why's the night dark? And why so far
the distance of the day?
sailor and fisherman say
to the navigable star.

Out there in billions, nodes of light
admit no questions, yet
their endless nuclear fret
for query is a kind of sight

whose radiance is everywhere
and indiscriminate –
extends, traverses, but
can't reach the eye its atoms share.

When Newton inked the paradigm
its huge magnetic roar
could leave no After or Before.
Still, darkness in the sky is time.

Curlew

What'll it be like, and how much time
will you have to remember, when the day goes loose
and breath won't come? How will memory trade
in the contracts of skin or the committee minutes
or the lurid headline or the off-colour joke
in a mouth full of tar in a pub on the road
all those years ago, all those years ago?

When air's taken and days spring apart
you'll go back for an instant, into the keeping
of the place you started: a wave on the boat,
and in the tarn's oxygen the fish restive;
steady the rod-hand; let the squall pass over.
A single curlew dripping tense into the sky,
and the whole sky momentarily weeping.

Bananas

You used to buy big hands of bananas
from the village shop. Every second day
your list-routine would pass his window.
Sometimes there'd be a book, cover upward,
thankless trash; and always cigarettes;
pill bottles; inhalers, upright;
and on the tablecloth weeks' worth of ash.

Never used to wave, no smile
offered, acknowledgement exchanged.
Eyes were the days shrunk, the window,
every second day the same: bananas,
list, ash, pills, trash, watched
from out of the dark; shopping and dying.

From the commodities that made the street
no applause, and in the end just air
and a newly washed tablecloth to tell
which one had given up, who wasn't trying.

Black Tulips

The tulip simultaneously retained its associations of precious treasure
yet was a prize in some form within reach of the common man.
For a modest outlay he could be drawn into the nexus of buying
and selling which, like all gambles, became quickly addictive.
Simon Schama, *The Embarrassment of Riches*, 1987 (1991), p. 351

The tulips speculated, lost their heads,
petal by petal undid their crowns.
At Keukenhof shorn rows tire out the day.
Bulbs trade like blood-lines. Everything dies.
A blackbird sings for summer coming loose.

Tulips can't speculate, and birds don't sing.
Days can't get tired. The carnival you see
you made, to name the atoms building air –
purpose ascribed to a performing vein.
A blackbird riddles early summer's bough.

There's money in this, true. But is there worth?
Bulbs trade like blood-lines, everything dies:
that hint of purple is investment's pride.
Nothing could make it wholly black, except
the blackbird riddling summer coming loose.

It's not the thing you see, it's how you see
the process gambling its belief alive.
Staked alike, nothing chooses not to be.
In this economy of colour, you,
and a blackbird's ritual for its singing tree.

Ithaka

He asked for a passage to Ithaka
at the wrong season of the year.
With all its magnetism leased
the compass was neither West nor East.
There's no Ithaka, insisted the needle North.
No Ithaka, mumbled the reluctant South,
No Ithaka here.

He asked for the way to Ithaka
from the city drunks and the winter snows.
It'll cost, sighed the traffic to a passer-by.
It'll cost, choked the bottle, and began to cry.
It'll cost, said the petals of a steel flower
to the credit card, that had just bought an hour
with a Christmas rose.

He invented a route to Ithaka
out of a trinket he found in the street.
A shop-window mannequin mopped its brow
with a hamburger wrapper stained with here and now.
You won't go far on that, my dear –
just as long as it takes you won't take a year.
And think of the heat.

He looked on the ring-road for Ithaka
but the signposts had strayed, or turned into thorn,
and the only maps were fragments of prayer.
Our Father, said the ages of anywhere.
Our Father, said the riddle of the lover's letter.
Our Father, said the zenith, *but it would have been better*
if you'd never been born.

He consulted the grammars for Ithaka.
That is my country, he thought, *with its long*
declensions, its morphology of time,
its optative mood and its poems that don't rhyme.
That is my country, and I'll make it exist.
But an older voice began to insist
that the grammars were wrong.

He bought all the guidebooks to Ithaka,
but the relevant pages had been torn away.
People always do that, said the bookseller's smile.
You could call the Helpline. But the telephone dial
connected him with a harassed priest
who knew nothing of Ithaka. *Not in the least.*
Where *did you say?*

He indexed the small ads for Ithaka,
found no one who went by the name.
Two Roxannes, an Amanda, and a private address
promised magical journeys, but nevertheless
they were bored by Ithaka. *Isn't it Greek?*
Hey, lover, same time, same place next week.
Glad that you came.

Time happened, as he looked for Ithaka –
into the different gardens thirty years of hail
fell and melted; the decades of birdsong
strewed the Zodiac, migrating among
its annual amendment; green came and went.
No point blaming time, time's innocent.
But nor is it frail.

Four consecutive passports for Ithaka.
He squinted from photographs, each of them bad.
On the first a young man trying to look old.
On the second a teller who wouldn't be told.
On the third the worrier, whose symptoms were cash.
And the fourth's stare narrowed through stubble and ash
at what Ithaka had:

Ithaka paid for the gate and the ticket
whose music was paper and comb.
It sponsored the needle, found the needle erratic,
the anaesthetist watching a mess of static;
the inhaler at the bedside; the gardens frozen.
And only Ithaka to grieve for the life it had chosen
that couldn't be home.

A Tourist on Waterlooplein

The last time we were here they were playing the samba
and cigar smoke creased round the stallholder's wrist
and the cafés sold incense and lucky stones.

Although it was early March, it was warm enough
those afternoons to sit outside and drink coffee
and the sun bloomed briefly in the waters of the Snoeksteeg.

Elsewhere the crowds, with their sum of unreliable accents,
queued for Anne Frank and the coinage of memory.
I'm sick of representations, you said. *Too expensive*

to buy off the darkness with a borrowed spring.
I thought a great deal about that form of mutilation –
famine in the cellar, while on the street

the compulsory grind of accordion music
constructed an occupation called loneliness.
It was too close to you, that imaginary self.

You preferred the samba, the Brazilian spices,
while every second train ran on schedule to Drenthe
and the sun bloomed briefly in the waters of the Snoeksteeg.

Perhaps tomorrow can be bought with a lucky stone.
Today burns slowly, hanging ash on the incense stick.
The first tulips are an intricate diversion.

You can't reconstruct yourself, it's too hard to remember
where you were, and how you got lost in the meanwhile.
*The last time we were here…*Well, it was as it was.

The Night Visitor

They're strange, the footsteps in the snow.
They lead four paces from the back door, stop
under the security light. Night
in the unlit brazier and the herb bed.
Then they vanish – the prints, I mean.
There's just snow, and a hemisphere of weather
where the garden's going smooth. You'd think
there'd be some trace of coming back,
shoes turning round in the dark.
You'd think... Well, no.
Four footsteps outward, then the night.
You had nowhere else to go.

The February Fences

When there's a big wind from the south-west
the garden
                    tilts. February
is moss and rain and non-alignment.

The fences, for example, all February
lean from the south-west,
inch by inch distorting the garden.
You can't put them back into alignment

however much you faff about in the garden
with plugs and hammers. It's February,
Atlantic weather and the south-west,
lattices and uprights out of alignment.

The discipline is the snowdrops at the back of the garden.
They know nothing of alignment or even February,
or how its fences encroach on the garden from the south-west.

They hang frail hoods against the weather,
It's not even a question of learning what to do.
It's because of the leaning rain, the non-alignment.
They have no angles. Therefore they are true.

Summer Sundays

On Sundays in the summer
the racing cars drive again into the distance
and in the beautiful gardens
the birdsong slowly falls silent.
The shops are so shut you can hear the church clocks strike.
For lunch there's the bafflement of not working.

The roar of aeroplanes falls gently into the gardens,
but the sun-loosened flowers can still hear the church clocks strike.
Perhaps that's why the birdsong slowly falls silent:
it's listening to the engines driving the summer
past the shut shops and into the distance
where no one's working.

Because no one's working
there are ambient noises in the neighbouring gardens:
an electric saw, a hammer, the coals of summer
being lit on a barbecue three fences in the distance.
The birch trees flush green, and are silent.
Perhaps the pit-crew has gone on strike.

How much longer, how much more silent
the birdsong will be as it vanishes into the distance.
In the distance it may never be summer
and all the engines won't think of working.
They'll be listening to the hours strike
at the shops, the birdsong in the gardens.

Time is what happens in adjacent gardens
whose grace is brief – a hammer-tap – and then is silent.
It's where things are going – the distance
where there's no birdsong and the only thing working
is racing cars overtaking the summer.
But how to determine the summer, when the clocks don't strike?

In that landscape the flowers aren't working.
There's ash on the driving-gloves, ash in the distance.
There's no birdsong. The clocks never strike.
There will never again be winter or summer.
There was no point working on the beautiful gardens
that are no longer beautiful despite being silent.

Counting the Lightning

The dog's in the garden chewing stones.
The tax demand lies on the table.

The washing-up – a supper for one –
can wait till morning. On the back step

you stand counting the lightning's distance.
Bees creep into tongues of the foxglove.

One-twenty. Two-twenty. Three-twenty...
The dog eats earth in the rain. The storm

is ample gunfire, siege of Schiphol.
The ashtray's drowned in the Atlantic.

One-twenty. Two- ... You could call it home,
such weather, its visible timing,

its intimate pressure. And you'll write
the gift of its diamonds in diamonds.

Geese at Vinkeveen

Do not concern yourself with the form of pain
                                    Dante, *Purgatorio* X

Spring and autumn it's Limbo –
cat civet staining
the spears of the crocuses;
a magpie wiping its beak against the lawn;
switching on and switching off
the hosepipe and the community fountain;
and there are the geese at Vinkeveen.

Their sky has been no civil enclosure.
The clouds wished for by fishermen
are simply the bringers of magnetism.
The magnificent sunset and the appearing moon,
filigree of isobars on the weather-map,
have no point beyond a form of digestion,
the compulsion of metal and oxygen.

Year after year, century after century,
and not knowing punishment as punishment!
Strangers saw flint-heads, sword-shafts,
ploughshares, constellations, omens, runes.
The geese saw themselves, and were themselves
forever, whose tragedy of breeding insists
that in the end no brood, nor even sentience, remains.

No redemption in this clamour on the sky.
There are only the old migration routes,
smell of the compass, instincts to repeat –
fifty millennia, never to make a soul.
Autumn's inverted taste is spring, the unfreezing
of karst and tundra. Unbiddably high,
five hundred geese fly north, and become coal.

An Epitaph

Once they were completed, my works
meant little to me –
old thoughts that quite by accident
thought through me.
And yet you will be reading them, somewhere –
grateful to be there.
Your earnest, friend, is admirable.
I still
won't care.

The Fat Girl

The fat girl's drinking diet stuff.
She thinks E-numbers make you thin,
imagines if she sinks enough
she'll have a life, and get a chin.

She wonders will she stud her tongue?
Perhaps one day she'll join the police.
What's bad for her is being young,
craving for skin, growing on grease.

Drummed into her by buffalo wings:
No one will love you if you're fat.
And true, her world of everythings
shrinks into loneliness. That's that.

The Wooden Bird

The wooden bird alighting by the pond
Has broken wings.
It aimed too distantly, too far beyond
The powers of its rusting springs.

No migration now, nor feather-beat.
No fret or mate.
The ice could finish it, or July heat.
No funeral's appropriate.

Smoke from the Vatican

The 265th Papal Election was concluded on 19 April 2005

Was it white? Was it black?
Or something in between?

Thoughts of the very much has-been
Leaked from a chimney-stack,

Were neither black nor white.
You couldn't really tell

Until the Sistine bell
Began to toll

For history, whose spite
And pity burn

Neither to white nor black,
But to the grey

Hard to discern

That never comes wholly back;
That won't go wholly away.

Birdsong

Nine months and you riddled the birds:
increasing song, then no song, then
the little spring. You lay awake
at six, whose world was listening:

blackbird and thrush; constriction in
a tree – called magpie; throat of wren.
Almost it could be April, but
lesser, with the migrants gone.

And you, among the dwindling voices,
whose power fails. Winter comes on,
brief flushes of late colour; snow's
nine petals in a box of nails.

Fado

During the raid, the fado
escaped from the brothel, crawled

along the docks: blood
flowering into rain-water; a shred of leather

on the edge of a diamond; rose petals
from the bedside bowl disfiguring

the surface of poison in a glass;
future of midnight a rosary of sirens.

A moment of emotion is the structure
of a cry with blood in its throat.

By dawn the local tragedy's locked up
but its meaning is still at large –

a girl wiping off her make-up; bruises as icons
whose names are becoming songs

repeating, repeating, changing
and remembering until all

the urban disasters have the purpose
of saints, the windows are unbroken,

and the terrible facsimiles of failure and love
have become love.

The Gravy People

Cheap cuts of meat after the war – tripe and lights
And eking out. Making do. It was almost a style.
And we were gravy people.
Without the gravy nothing was a meal.

And eking out? Making do, that was the style:
Half a pound of butter and a sewing kit.
But without gravy nothing was a meal.
After a while you made the best of it.

Half a pound of butter and a sewing kit.
You'd never think we'd won a war.
After a while you made the best of it.
There was so much you just learned to ignore.

You'd never think we'd won the war.
For years we queued for stamps to feed the ration book.
There was so much you just learned to ignore.
If you complained you got a funny look.

For years we kept those stamps up in the ration book.
The best was cod and chips.
No one complained. You'd get a funny look.
There were no pretty clothes. And as for foreign trips…

The best was once a month, those cod and chips.
Apart from that… Cigarettes, and lard.
You wanted pretty clothes, or seaside trips,
But soon forgot them, and it wasn't hard.

We won the war on tea and cigarettes and lard,
On patience, mending, knowing not to feel.

And lights, or tripe? They make a lovely meal.
It wasn't hard. We were gravy people.

After Beowulf

Tall trees seething; torchlight of larch
lashing, then extinguished; long the darkness
flaring at midday; fatal the wind's way.

Air smells of metal. All must be stowed,
bulwark of boat brought dry to land.
Bitter such breast-care, how brief the burning.

A pyre must be placed, its precious cargo,
his death-songs made ready to rinse memories.
Residues, witness... This is the wreck of time:

Future has failed him, features are melting
now no one knows, needs to recall them.
They turn into tricks, are trash; are ash.

Become, what will become? Claws beyond rush-brand,
ripped perimeters. On Hronesness
he has gone to goodbye to get an answer

while the gale is unmaking gods and funerals.
We shall light more relics. Yet this, the last contest
drained out of days, whose deal of farewell

is unsteadying all flame...

From West of Eden

I

Pumice. Ridges of old lava
Littered with scorpions.
Barbed wire that guards
A minefield whose maps are lost.
A valley floor, disputed
By buses   dust   wind
And at the edge of an eye
An eye, prisms of the sun.

II

Not that they wanted to stay.
Under the flags, the parade's kitsch,
The tarmac melts over
The plans for the unbuilt library
And locusts squabble quietly over
The juice of a road-kill.
The local elections were
Cancelled, ravished by visions.

III

The heat-haze is no place
For the civic virtues.
Laughter's absent, punishable,
And the only neighbours
Are envy, the various addictions,
Each insisting its god is love,
Coerced to rifle time
To call this home.

for clive   /s/   cott

                                 s   katers

in all thi   s

                                 s   lither

                  one   θ   ink

                                 s   of

     wordswor   θ

being pur   s   ued by

     manias in the   f   orm of mountains

('we hi   s   ed along the

        poli   ʃ   ed

           /aɪ   s/   ' etc.)

                             h   ere in the

     colde   s   t march

                               f   or

                               θ   irty years

                               h   olland

                               ʃ   arpens

           it   s   blades

crouches over the   s   pine of a

                               s   kate

           but thi   s   year the *el*

                               f

                               s   *tedentocht* is

                               s   ta

                               ʃ   ionary

though all the polders ru   ʃ   to the

               nor   θ

                 we   s   t

in the direction of gra   s   mere,

                fa   s

                     /t/

William of Normandy

The king's body burst
when the eight it took to lift him
tried to squodge him
into his sarcophagus.

The nave filled with a foul smell...
Eight ran away, squawking portents.

Riddle the entrails
of a hippopotamus:
when kings become extinct
thugs sniff an opportunity.

Perplexity

One's life's work – *dahlings*! It's going... mushy,
That ceremony of innocence well on the way
To being drowned.
One's publishers, you know... Wrote yesterday –
They were polite of course, not pushy –
To say it hadn't found
A readership, my work: *Stillborn* –
Unfortunately fluid blah – *Already being pulped* –
There are no grounds –
Etc. I must admit I gulped
While pocketing their cheque, drawn
For thirty pounds.

Witness

Undo the rope from the rafter, young lover,
Give the sunlight back its crutch.
Prise the note from its crack in the mortar
Old fingers can't touch.

Now take me down to the river, young lover,
And chill my lips with chalk.
Unclothe me, wash me in the cool water,
Then teach me to talk.

Sit me under the willow, young lover,
Where the leaves in the wind turn white.
Don't stay to listen. Head back to the slaughter
With your eyes full of spite.

You'll disappear for good, young lover,
No syllable prove you'd been there.
Time is the hands of the hangman's daughter,
And I am air.

III

Masterpieces

It was a curious experience, writing these poems. In 2001, for a variety of silly and complex reasons, I didn't think I would ever write verse again. In 2001, though, I was confronted for the first time with Jacob Maris's painting *De afgesneden molen* ('The Mill' in the texts below, although a literal rendering of the Dutch title would be something like 'The truncated windmill'). There in the Rijksmuseum I jotted down the phrase 'Elsewhere is ochre' in a notebook. After that, and for reasons I still don't entirely understand, I kept going back to the Rijksmuseum, merely in order to continue what had started as a dialogue with some paintings, had become a conversation with a culture, and had ended in... Who knows where such talks end? What I know certainly is that the paintings not only taught me to look, they also helped me to see, and in some strange way, urged me to listen, too. It was in the seeing and listening that these poems began. I hadn't intended to write them – I never went into the Rijks thinking 'Today I am going to write a poem about such-and-such a painting' – but I was glad to engage with the whole business of writing verse again. Sometimes I hung around in front of the paintings, feeling like a kind of stalker... and wrote nothing. At other times I made notes, usually of a very literal kind – about dimensions, or events that were happening off-centre in the paintings, about gestures, or apparently commonplace actions, that it might have been easy to overlook. Of course, the meanings I was looking at, and listening for, might not be the readers' meanings – everyone will read the paintings differently, just as they will these poems – but never mind. The paintings resist all attempts at appropriation, and insist on being themselves. Because of that open-endedness, that boundless integrity, what I felt when I was working on these poems was... generosity. Perhaps it's not only its technical brilliance, its principles of construction, its inevitable persistence, or even its semantic plurality, that allows us to judge any work of art 'great'. Generosity must also be reckoned with. And it is tolerant.

October 2004

The Mill

Jacob Maris, *De afgesneden molen*, 1872. Rijksmuseum, Amsterdam

Elsewhere is ochre, sombre
this crust of ice, your breath.

It's how the wind's cut:
horizontal. You're narrowing your eyes.

Your journey's been scraped
from monochrome. You've been flensed.

Already you're grudging the cold –
brambles stiff in the ginnel,

that smear of frost.
Darkness in daylight.

There's no one else on the road.
It's happening to you.

You're grease, surviving
these stricken provinces.

And shortly nightfall.
Nowhere left to go.

The Drinker

Frans Hals, *De vrolijke drinker*, c. 1628–30. Rijksmuseum, Amsterdam

He composes himself among the janitors,
flush of the security lights,
the smells of wax and yesterday –
for company.
Daybreak hurts.

You are the crowd of one for whom
he looks up, gestures, draws his lips –
for company.
A form of acknowledgement.
Your footsteps

like his rehearsed the children's funerals –
for company,
the no-pulse of the *ochtendmist*,
the sad processions, crêpe and lavender;
closed each fist.

A brilliant hangover? A trivial grief?
Failing to be surprised by what
your likeness wears, he smiles –
for company – since
you do not.

Woman Reading a Letter in Blue

Vermeer, *Brieflezende vrouw in het blauw*, 1663–64.
Rijksmuseum, Amsterdam

It's how in moments of crisis
you notice
the blue nape of the chairs,
the highly polished buttons
stitching the upholstery,
and completing one wall
the polders in tapestry.

And here she is, in the vertical
spaces of now, the debris
of a well-kept house –
so engrossed in the letter
she holds it in two hands.
One leaf's already through,
discarded. Elsewhere
light's collecting
on a string of pearls,
high-angled and blue.

Neither smiling nor unsmiling
she'll read this letter forever.

A moment sooner, and she would have been
too quickly taking off her coat.
A moment later, and she would have been
leaning on the table for support.

But it will always be now.
That child will never be born.

The Problem with Virtually any Self-Portrait

It's not the pose, the brilliant fury,
that obvious pathos in the rotting teeth,
the rubble of the penitent breast.
It's simply that the man beneath
was not one of your best.

The Bleaching Fields

Jacob van Ruisdael, *View of Haarlem from the north-west*, c. 1670.
Rijksmuseum, Amsterdam

From this dune-top the sun's south-east:
flushes of heat, wind in the rigs of the polder.
It could be nothing
but a late spring day, May's fast-moving
clouds, their shadows spreading on the bleaching fields,
and over Haarlem a drying sky.

What's the weather
but energy and entailment? Sun strikes
red pantile, and it's time to run the linen
at the edge of a textile town.
In the bleaching fields the flavour of lavender,
and over Haarlem a drying sky.

On last year's stubble
the linen goes stiff. Sparse trees slant eastwards
from prevailing weather. In the textile town
in the distance the masts of the church have nowhere to sail to.
Beyond the dunes and the bleaching fields
by Haarlem it's never quite warm.

Old Woman Reading

Rembrandt van Rijn's *An old woman reading* (*Lezende oude vrouw*, 1631)
is thought by some critics to be a representation of the prophet Anna.
Others think it is a representation of his mother Neeltgen (Nellie).
Rijksmuseum, Amsterdam

I told that child
he mustn't flatter. All that matters
is the Book, I said, God knows.

That headscarf
was braid of Leyden best, and gold-embossed.
The detail had to take him hours,

working the light thick
until it made a head and book that weighed
a dam of shadows. Still my right hand froze.

Some kind of rapt
arthritic gold. Inauthentic. Old.
The saints I read don't really look like that.

Besides, you can't make out
the words I had to touch. The Book's not even Dutch.
From what I saw, I only seem at ease.

He never tells me
what he makes. For all the prophets he can fake
I wish he'd do a Proper Job.

The Storm

Ludolf Bakhuyzen, *Ships in distress in heavy storm*, c. 1690.
Rijksmuseum, Amsterdam. The concluding quote is lifted directly
from the commentary on Bakhuyzen's painting as
found in the 2004 exhibition *The Masterpieces*.

However you see a blowsy seascape
he was trying for the epic
as a question of urgency
and how to do those waves.

That the North Sea has no dignity
and isn't Dutch? It is dirty and immortal.
It smashes ships as matters of technique.
Its surface trade is relics on the Scheldt.

Those waves aren't Protestant.
The drowning cries are what you get
for your money in this world, madam.
Of course our ambitions are matchwood.

You have never seen a painting
whose over-obvious waves so anxiously ask
*How mortal am I? Do you admire
how true to life I've been?
What will they say of me?*

They will say that *It is said
that in bad weather Bakhuyzen
often went out to sea.*

Fishing in the River of Souls

Adriaen Pietersz. van de Venne, *De zielenvisserij*, 1614.
Rijksmuseum, Amsterdam

We're fishing in the river of souls
again. Today
it's the Turk, the Croatians and the Poles
for whom we earnestly pray,

and yesterday it was the Jew,
again – except…
Except we don't think that was true.
Records weren't centrally kept.

Before the Jew it was the Black,
our contrary.
That smell of genesis and crack
was cheap. Eventually.

And before the Black, the Catholicks,
who weren't like us:
their scarlet enjoyments, candlesticks,
their gilt and *dominus* –

we fished them from the river of souls
with some distaste.
But in God's economy of wholes
nothing must go to waste.

So we still fish for souls. This week
we have applied
new tackles, an advanced technique –
efficient; unified.

The gibberish, the drowning cry,
the grappling hook:
our customs don't quite let you die.
And then we throw you back.

Skaters

Hendrick Avercamp, *Winter landscape with ice skaters*, c. 1609.
Rijksmuseum, Amsterdam

The sail was destined for a chocolate-box,
the capering village for a tin of tea.
Jackdaws clatter in the winter branches
while someone pisses under the same tree.

For all the activity – the hockey-sticks,
the boat-hooks jabbed at skates, the braziers, flame
below a window opened onto ice –
nothing is happening. There is no name

for how time has collapsed, how everyone
is urgently enjoying that present need
to chat or crap, to bully, scrape or chide
before they fade. Before they come to fade.

Happy Families

Jan Steen, *Het vrolijke huisgezin*, 1668. Rijksmuseum, Amsterdam

for Fergus Wilde

The Holy Family, whose name is Troost,
are getting pissed. The dog's on rubber legs,
the youngest slurps a touch, the shawm's on fire,
the frying-pan's on the floor... It missed the eggs.

The announcing angel's dangling his horn,
and through an opened window sucks a pipe.
The vat, the flute, the noise... The tablecloth's
askew to show the mother's breasts are ripe.

And underneath the cleavage, meat and bread,
cooked lamb whose moral is the Golden Age.
Its children play unsteadily in the dark.
Soo d'oude songen... Hanging from the page

that Steen's tacked prominently to the mantel
the future's greased. Its emblem is a dish
whose contents come to little in the end
but cheese and football, beer, and fat, and fish.

IV

Torquatus

Horace in the Sabine Hills

In this loneliness
I've noticed an inclination to address fragments of poems
To the plants in the garden, which thrive on the lyric gift
In this loneliness
And a tendency to harrumph, to mock, or to repine
At the dismantling of the things, places and people
Who used to make life bearable, and even fair
In this loneliness
Hanging around in a dirty old habit,
Lusting after the ladies who bring me the news,
Finding everything harder to finish,
And forgetting – though forgetting is also a mercy
In this loneliness
I'll probably end up admiring exotic trees
Or banging on about Empire, while at the back of my head
There's a little refrain of interest to no one except the unfinished poem
Whose nature is both incremental and exhausting.
Well, one has done one's best
In this loneliness
Perhaps I should advertise. The problem there is
One finds oneself becoming over-ordered, and I should imagine
That difficult to live with. And besides, I tried –
Only to find the structure deficient in those quantities
I managed with ease in the old days, and the hand
Always, and always unbidden, writing out the phrase
In this loneliness

A Letter to Torquatus

Frankly I don't know how you can stand it –
For months the same broken doors in the kitchen;
The relics of weeks-old meals on the bedspread;
Vitreous stains that haven't received due attention.
But perhaps after all a life should be measured
By the capacity for bearing what its critics call squalor,
And equally, perhaps it's merely over-fussy
Or prurient to find dirt somehow deficient,
Whereas clearly it's a symptom of long-drawn-out resentment
That begins in the classroom, ramifies through families,
Dispatches its lovers late at night to the wine-shops
And will drop its fag-ash even into the open palm
That has begun to beckon towards the final judgement.

You might take it, Torquatus, as a species of sympathy –
Though you'll see only nit-picking antiquity
And tell me robustly to mind my own business.
Quite right. A man so lonely
That for company he murmurs at saplings
Or drones over-loudly about the dubious merits
Of olive oil or sea-bathing
Has no right to engage with the intricate choices
Of others. Still… How many decades, between us?
Truth is I've admired your insouciance
In the face of time and non-being,
And the years have allowed me, down to dust and atoms,
To compose the lineaments of order, called friendship.

I will look for your smile even as my monologue
Makes the women fall asleep in their soup-plates.
You will look for my approval among a chaos of nurses.
We shall slip into the dark out of step, but hand in hand.

The Boy

Why so cut up? From the beginning the boy
Wasn't suitable, wasting your time and your talents.
And the remedy isn't, as you seem to imply,
Chasing after the nearest stray piece of Etruscan skirt.
But who hasn't been there? Been stricken, begging
Time to stand still, the face we created come back?
Nevertheless, beyond a certain age this becomes... unbecoming.
After all we know that once the door's slammed
The candles will eventually resume their poise, and work
Be able to wrest some little beauty
From a world whose disorders seem depressingly constant.
No point studying your reflection in a glaze of maudlin.
Better to regard one's crows'-feet as hallmarks of polity.

Your invocations of myth... They make me impatient.
Consider. The gods are stripped of quotidian
Muddle. Your Orpheus, for instance: hard to imagine
That profound singer with haemorrhoids, gingivitis,
A phobia about the transmission of avian diseases,
Or in the gathering shades worrying about the set of his toupee.
Instructive they may be, these stylisations
Divested of laughter, and yet to confuse
Such serious imagos with our mortal riot –
To imagine we're them, garbed in their same gestures –
Is to think we can live sanely and happily
On the snows of Olympus. Torquatus, Olympians
We're not (I add only, Thank goodness).

Therefore take heart, despite your cloudy abstraction.
And this metaphor, heart? It's a question of cultivation.
I doubt you'll find the best of what's left of that vulnerable organ
In the bedroom, nor yet in the amphora's seductive compulsions,
But perhaps, if you're lucky, on a pause in the journey
Whose unequal struggles we're alike enduring,
Worn out with patience; whose Farewells have been said.

Poppies

In our chalk and on a south-facing slope the poppies
Thrive, Torquatus, in the sunshine so lacking in reticence
That their mouths open everywhere like the beginnings of
                                        exclamation,
And without treatment the vines would be interrupted by their gossip.
There are those who love them, who see them as benison
Or drug alike, who collect them by the armful.
Time was, I did so myself, walking summer's hedgerows
Pleased with their gaudy if only because its abundance
Meant a pestle and crushed seed, the fumes of nightfall
Whose lovely forgetting paused even the gods' interventions
And gave the diurnal ambitions a moment of respite.
Yet one's proclivities alter. What was once craving
Becomes merely impatience in the face of the profligate.

Busy. The poppies are far too busy
With their own replication, garish, prolific –
That flamboyancy, that craving for attention…
Vulgarity. Too much reminiscent of the *demos*, the forum,
Whose stupendous clamour – I have whispered it, know its
                                        attractions –
Is for all to be made forever equal, all talents
The same, that none shall ever be overlooked, nor forgotten.
Yet the slaves still choke in the dust of the circus.
Is it age, Torquatus, that drives one to value
The most difficult savour, not respite but repose?

Rather, I think, the kitchen garden, whose stubborn herbs
Have at least some medicinal virtue, are quieter,
And are happy to be tended among lavender and myrtle;
Or vines, whose pruning must be no less artful
If the grape's to be sweet enough to appease Bacchus.
At my lifetime, you see, one appreciates a view –
However colourful, however lucrative or spectacular –
Much less than the flavour of a useful digestive.

Verbena

...pulling faces. And extraordinary expedients
such as reciting their verses inside the ribs of a barrel
(they call this amplitude)
or declaiming reams of sub-Homeric rubbish
while standing one-legged on top of a pillar
(they call this projection)...

...I call them unfortunate, whose talents
have found no reliable patron,
no intelligent audience.
So much of their gift will have to be squandered
to the gawp of sensation, out of whose mouth...
...unreliably echoed...

...cannot bear silence. Precisely at those moments
one learns how to listen to the past which
still in its schoolroom
recites the structure of its envies, its failures
ever to please, its discovery of excuses,
rote of evasions...

...one doesn't blame them. But they're mistaken –
decline into rivals and begging, the more bitter
the smaller the talent,
as sparrows quarrel over a seed in the dung
dropped by the emperor's horse only
minutes earlier...

...I have set out verbena. After this winter
the ground's still reluctant. There are days
without visitors;
of thin easterlies and incipient frost.
Autumn in May, blossom draining
from the limbs of cherry...

Bed

I have this urge
To run out naked on the roads
And scream.

Instead
I climb back into bed,

Whose silent customs
The gods will not revile, nor yet
Redeem.

March in June

More like June in March, Torquatus;
More like March in June.
Brass cracks in the summer frost, blood
Melts from the winter moon.

Armies on the Tigris scorch
Where cold unravels fire.
Storms, indifferent to harbours, shrink
Sails into hissing wire.

Among all this, you write to say
The girl betrayed, the cup
Of sorrow's therefore wholly spilled?
Take heart. And do grow up.

Trade

Come off it, Torquatus. That rich bitch
may well have made
the room seem luminous, but she
turned sex to trade –

even when tongues turned ugly
and licked her dregs…
Rumour himself couldn't withstand her
when she opened her legs.

You're well out of it, man. Think.
Better to behave
as if she'd never existed
than live like a slave.

And better by far that quieter love
that will embrace you
at the edge of shadows; forgive you,
not deface you.

Days

To be hurt by the world,
Torquatus – the unsolid
Friendships, the spoiled
Envies, all that failed

Of effort or surprise –
Is only to find what lies
Crippled by real days
In any child's eyes.

Not to want to play;
To take back the toy;
To sulk; to turn away:
Manners of a boy.

Harder to choose to live
With just enough, leave
One's friends to other love,
And be forgotten, gruff

With too long of loneliness.
Nevertheless
It's in this ancient place
That days bring grace,

Whose only proper attitude
Is to try to be glad
We once had what we had,
Not that we did what we did.

Ochre

Striving, Torquatus:
the incessant hiss
of endless busyness.
You seem to simmer

in a world of scrolls,
anxious among patrons,
steaming at each hint
of distance or dislike –

a heat-haze
disfiguring the great
while the crowd's every commonplace
gesture trembles.

Here it's full summer,
so much dust in the sky
that the burnt moon rises
in all its ochres…

…She is the last of my loves,
patient, imperious.
I am slowly unburdened
where her appraisal dances –

old enough to know
that to get where you want to go
then it's usually necessary
to begin somewhere else.

Sherbet

Hard to know exactly how to respond, Torquatus,
to the oddballs and sects –
those gazes maddened by seeing
gods in the desert's glare;
the wretched ebonies, diseased, hangdog,
drifting in from Nubia;
the circus of those who believe in the filth
of their bodily resurrection.

I try to imagine, on a good day,
that they may have something to teach us,
but among their stench of insistence
that's as difficult as believing
a non-compliant animal should not be whipped.

All the same, to those perpetually thirsty
there seems little point saying *We*
have engineers, we
have aqueducts, we
have a theory of water. We
have no real intention of breaking our nails,
and that alabaster is finally exquisite…
Such manners only make them resentful.

Better that slaves are set to doing tricks
on the scorched earth,
are torched, parched merely by time,
while we sit by our swimming-pools
and watch heat hiss past in sherbet.

The Senator

Broke that winter, avoided
as if I were an unlucky place.
I've not forgotten
that those among whom I'd served so long,
for whom I served,
saw only my disgrace.

I walked the city, trying to reconcile
the fading of my given name
with the civic statues,
who looked the other way. Ducks fussed
at slush in aqueducts. What
after all was fame?

I gave up hope of messages,
sat in the kitchens of a thinned estate,
listened to slaves.
Perhaps that was the afterlife, where
time happens, the dice are chanceless,
and it's getting late.

A Reply to Virtue

Virtuous men, Torquatus? Beware alike
the implicit claim, the extended context –
and don't include me.

Indeed I have failed at virtue, whose vice
has been to attribute too much intelligence,
too much integrity

to those I thought I liked. And still
I have only to look at a woman's smile,
have only to see

an imperious nod of her head, feel
the touch of an exploratory hand,
and I'm lost.

Suspended in time and judgement, I
have not been virtuous. Or if that was virtue,
this is its cost.

Raking

They don't pause with their rakes. They just go on,
Garden after garden,
In a culture of scraping away
The winter moss, last of the rain.

Never to look up, never to deflect
The troublesome cataract
From blade or tine: stiff concentration
Learned early, a way to survive –

Whose names underwrote armies which sieve dirt
For roads in a desert,
Navies which tumble off the edge of the world.
It's all beyond them, has become uncertain:

Why did we neaten sand? How do the sails
Fill when the ship falls?
Was it for good? Ah, once... But once,
Like gold-embossed ivory, is too long ago.

They're us, Torquatus – old men exiled, filching
A few years from their scratching,
Handles of tools gone smooth in their fingers;
Brittle; hurt in sudden chills.

Does better exist?... *hell with it.* Just to go on,
Knowing not to be born
Is best... The rest is bent misfortune,
Raking the scurf of winter from the lawn.

Roads

Let us have no religions, Torquatus, except those which belong
To roads and libraries, to a code of manners whose primary purpose
Is the maintenance of parks and fountains. In such belonging,
Whose polity is the most artful avoidance of shame,
At least one's loneliness can be stroked by civic duty
While being soothed by old architectures in public gardens.
No need, in that context, to invent a wood,
Sacred or otherwise, where some shit-smeared seeress
Rants tearfully about the magic properties of acorns
Or the glass-spindled blood-sword that will choose the slain
And fetch them to the messy and exhaustive deflowering
Of virgin rivers, where ululation is unfortunately compulsory.
Such enthusiasm leads merely to nothing to read:
Their runes of grief are all very well, but such
Over-simplicity, one finds, is the better confronted
If there's a definite place in which to dawdle, or better yet,
A comfortable spot at which to sit down.

By the Germans' keenness for meaning discovered
In the bowels of sacrifice I'm left disconcerted.
What to make of the Semnones, whose pubic hairs
Are hallowed by auguries? The Idisi, whose horses' entrails
Unbind any fetters? The Chatti, who ritually deflesh
Their priests and pour libations through a skull's colander
In order to secure from the crudities of the heavens
Not, as one might expect, a bountiful crop of asparagus
But an assurance that their enemies shall soon be visited
By a plague of – of all things – frogs? Such fundamentalism
Can't, of course, endure teasing, and is therefore
A fit subject only for gawps or the circus.
Yet are we, Torquatus, havering among scrolls,
So very different? I suppose we are. It's why I write
Of roads and libraries, since it's only on the civilised journey
That one can cultivate any sense of the erotic, and only
Among books that posterities can in their ruin share
Their spoiled democracy of post-coital sadness.

Still, and finally, we're distinguished from the barbarian
By the fact that their depressions are so dismally local:
A circle of beech-leaves; a resentful mere
Whose brood is monstrous; a pitiful altar
Insisting that its broken stones are somehow animate;
Brittle braids of hair adapted as amulets
To appease the fingers of drowned girls in river-pools...
Our Mercury, at least, implies that distances exist,
That trade must travel, that engineers, cartographers
Never need be unemployed. Besides which, of course,
Any theory of maps must involve the exploitation
Of edges – not the sulks of the oracle, but strategy,
Whose pointer, scratching at the calm of the library, obliterates
Exclusively, and after due reflection. It's there, in that tactical
Pause, that she must slowly disrobe, there
Slave watch incuriously while skin is bitten in the name
Of pleasure, there good alliance determine the future –
Whose roads make our verses, our measured syllables
Which else couldn't be told from indiscriminate sobbing.

On a Request for New Material

New songs, they said. *The old no longer please.*
Give us the sort of... stuff... that will appease
Augustus... By which they mean not to appease
Augustus, but to please the rabble trying to appease
Augustus. And to these friends I can only say
Augustus is never to be pleased.

Time was, lifetimes ago, when the heroic boom
Or elegiac subtlety came easy, measured
Only by an over-developed gift for showing off.
To challenge, change, or none the less confirm –
For three decades that was my trade.
And yes, I pleased Augustus. I was seldom paid.

Fashions, the too-much-indulged? Don't talk to me of how
The insistence on one civic madness is eclipsed
By yet another silliness, merely on the nod
Of a consul's horse, or entrails of a toad.
The insistence turns squalid, its lines grow out of date,
Augustus out of temper, live at a whim made late.

And now, having pleased Augustus, written out and far
From anywhere, what's left of words and life intends
Merely to cherish and protect. Dear I hold
The faces of friends, a space of peace, a house
Resentment and the world can rarely enter. How,
Therefore, should I write to please Augustus,
Again submit to judgement in the slums
Of time? New songs? I'd rather grow
Vegetables. The answer's No.

The Peon Rose

I've cast as crooked an eye, Torquatus, on my fellows
As they on me.
To appease this one? A wink, suasion. We might agree…
Or not agree;
To sell that one's taste, or buy her mother? I'd seem *engagé*,
Witty or abrupt,
The whole show – standing there like a fool under the fountain of
pleasure
With my hands cupped.

And yet Augustus is never to be pleased, the usual crowd
Drinks far too much,
And at the core of the peon rose there's a stem of ice
Which time can't touch –
Not even time, whose power forced so much loneliness that
I had to make
Imaginary friends, like a child, from our catalogue of errors
Where hearts can't break;

Not even time, that brings to grief alike the gullible and
The innocent,
Can melt the promise frozen in the petal's complexity.
And is the intent
Of being old to warn, or to laugh, that this shall happen?
Or well to rage
That sex will chill on the fondest, most agile lips – bored stiff,
Unsalved, by age?

My dear old friend, what conceivable use are we here,
Exiled or lost?
These days I prefer slaves' company. Each love comes slowly,
Each has its cost.
Time stains our breath, the bowl of the wine-pitcher is
A shadow in dust.
It's turning cold. It's crooked to write on, another mere folly.
And yet I must.

Sand

Time to move on, Torquatus –
Leave the fond hopes sweating behind.
Their infinite futures were squalors –
Merely illusions, in an illusory mind.

Our time? A foetor, a fever.
Its end should be managed without fuss.
Tears are inappropriate
For its patients, since they are us.

I looked at the kitchen garden;
Heard an unaccustomed voice
Break into the silence
Of emptied rooms… This choice

Was heartbreaking, and it was mine…
It's a matter of how to behave –
Trying to go on with work,
Refusing to live like a slave…

It's only a desert, my dear,
Whose glare is intricate schemes
Infecting the light with dreams.
Yet sand claims us, and smothers the dreams.

The Visitor

We've become the old lot, Torquatus –
Wrong-headed, in the antique clothes and postures
Intended to manage the ludicrous attitudes
Of an allegedly more primitive century.
We simply appear risible to those
Who can't imagine our frets and urgencies
Were remarkably like theirs, our erections
And deceits alike no less pressing,
Our civic monuments no less contemporaneous,
Our gardens no less utilitarian
(And often more sheerly beautiful), our libraries
No less incredible or extensive, our kindness
Occasionally no less surprising.
Meanwhile and everywhere

There are those who want to know how they can help,
And those who want to know whom they should sue;

Those who feel responsible,
And those who feel resentful;

Those who know it's occasionally nice to be silent,
And those who must have everything spelled out;

Those who are temporarily discomfited,
And those who insist on being permanently aggrieved.

A pity. I've spent most of the morning
Standing uselessly in the courtyard, muttering
At no one, struggling with the standard unforgiving
Compulsions, with both fists clenching –
An absurd exile from a time turned embarrassing.
But somewhat unusually I am expecting
A visitor. While she talks about nothing
I shall imagine her undressing,
And I shall forget all this, and everything.

The Vinegar Days

for Grevel Lindop

Do you too wince, Torquatus – and if so, with aversion
Or reluctant affection? – as you remember the days
Left standing in vinegar, the vinegar days?
Hours of failed strategy, the foreplay to… to what?
The seduction from which one woke with a start
Having drooled on her shirt?
After the diplomatic handshake, turning away
From one's over-suave host into the evening
And then on the serenely raked path smiling
(One hopes with indulgence) at the climacteric
Of frotting groans and squeaks spawned
From the dark back of barbed wire at the yard's end
Where someone was had, and the other done?
Nights when the vine was the imaginary friend
One clutched for support in the taxi home
As one wept – how one wept! – for Rome?

They were vinegar days, and those supple,
Those abstemious, those cunning, less literal –
Those riddling their remaining senatorial lock
Too carefully across their crowns, those speaking
For effect in unfamiliar accents, the declamatory fools –
They warned us, or didn't warn us,
And have taken our places.
Of those gentle, those unconvinced – the best are gone
With the work unfinished, translated
Into a place where neither you nor I can pose.
The taxis no longer ply down the line of lights.
Sombre-eyed, fussy, still occasionally somewhere wheeled on
Like some unholy relic to cant something almost sensible,
I glance at fifty – abrupt, beaten, indefensible.

And here, in the flat, assumptive province
Called exile it's been autumn since winter. Although
The volumes have been alphabetised and a fire lit,

For months the house has been tossed in dry northerlies,
Familiar plants are early stripped, and the damaged leaf
Is burned with last year's paperwork to scurf.
No one told me that I'd have to learn
Such competence with grief.
I stare out, walk, take random routes, remembering
How happy… How hopeless… *The vinegar days.*
Only to my dearest friends, I write –
Usually to find them partly dismantled or wholly gone away –
While the white wind raves across the whitening clay.